Words of Fucking Wisdom
A Journal for

the Spirited Soul

MIMI MARGARITA

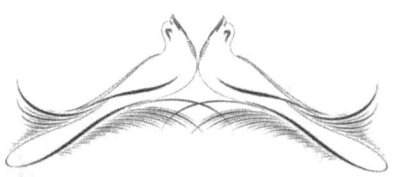

This journal belongs to:

THERE'S ALWAYS ANOTHER BEGINNING TO CARRY ON AND LIVE FUCKING AWESOME!

PUBLISHED BY WINDSURF PUBLISHING LLC
GREENWICH, CT
COPYRIGHT © 2023 WINDSURF PUBLISHING LLC
ISBN: 978-1-936509-32-4

ALL RIGHTS RESERVED. NO PART OF THIS BOOK MAY BE REPRODUCED, STORED IN A RETRIEVAL SYSTEM, OR TRANSMITTED IN ANY MEANS, ELECTRONIC, MECHANICAL, PHOTOCOPYING, RECORDING, OR OTHERWISE, WITHOUT THE PERMISSION OF THE PUBLISHER.

DISCLAIMER: THE AUTHOR AND PUBLISHER OF THIS JOURNAL MAKES NO CLAIMS THAT THE CONTENTS OF THIS BOOK CAN OR SHOULD TAKE THE PLACE OF THERAPY FROM A LICENSED PROFESSIONAL IF NEEDED. THE JOURNAL IS INTENDED FOR ENTERTAINMENT PURPOSES ONLY AND SHOULD BE REGARDED AS SUCH. IT IS THE RESPONSIBILITY OF THE JOURNAL OWNER TO MAKE THAT DETERMINATION IF ANY AND ACT RESPONSIBLY. WITH THAT SAID, MAY YOU ENJOY THIS ADULT JOURNAL FOR THE SOUL. - WINDSURF PUBLISHING LLC

About This Journal

Hello, let's get off to a great fucking start here. It's really simple. Sometimes we get disappointed or pissed off at people or life situations, and rightfully so. Thus, this journal is a place to give you an opportunity to let out your emotions from feeling afraid, belittled, taken, slighted, and treated badly by others. It's an opportunity to vent, to get things off your chest, let go of past anger, frustration, and any fucking unhappiness. It's also a place to think of the happiness you do have and what you can look forward to in life. It's to help you think about your inner thoughts and situations, feeling yourself fully, and reflect on what has happened to you. Perhaps this will help you happily grow and know yourself all the better to move forward. It may make you laugh or cry. Yet, its all geared to help you take yourself and your power back. So sit still and write all about you. Let everything hang out freely and feel the emotions that they bring. Embrace them and get to know yourself better. Think of how you can have a greater life with new awareness, beginnings, or endings. You deserve a happy life and the fuck best! Remember, your thoughts help you to create the magic in your life. Peace always, Mimi

Decide to love yourself more fully than fuck before with new intentions for a better life

What are some ways you can show more love to yourself? Write about it below and make some new plans. Don't let anything get in your way.

Be your own
fucking
best friend

What are ways you are already your own best friend? What are ways you could be? Describe.

It's best to
listen to your
inner voice
and
forget the people
who are
fucking creeps

What does your inner voice often tell you? Write about some of your most intimate thoughts.

Simply tell obnoxious people you don't like to put up or shut up. Don't take their fucking shit!

When were there times when you had to tell people to stop talking or shut up? Why did you and what did that feel like?

When was a time you wanted to take back your power from a jackass? What did you do?

Never let
a fucking
jackass make
rules for you
or tell
you what
to do

Take the time to make a list of things that you know are important to yourself right now.

Decide on what's really fucking important for you

Do not let the opinions of others fuck up your head

Remember a time (s) when you let other people's opinions influence your thoughts in negative ways.

Spend the majority of your time with people who make you feel fucking great and valued

Who are the people in your life that add to your experiences in positive ways, make you feel good, and valued? Write some things about them.

Make each day fucking matter

What are ways you can make "every day" matter more to make your life happier in general?

Give yourself a great fucking spa day soon

Take time to self love at a spa. Write about the things you can do there for yourself and when.

Confirm your confidence with courageous affirmations every fucking day

What courageous affirmations can you think of to build up your self confidence and courage?

Never ask an asshole a good question and expect a good answer

Listening to yourself is far better than listening to an asshole. Write about times you listened to yourself and the difference it made for you.

Don't take advice from fucking jerks

If someone pretends to be a friend but really means to harm you and gives you garbage advice, how will you handle the situation?

Never let an asshole insult who you are and get the fuck away with it

Remember a time when you were embarrassed and insulted by someone just plain mean. Describe the experience.

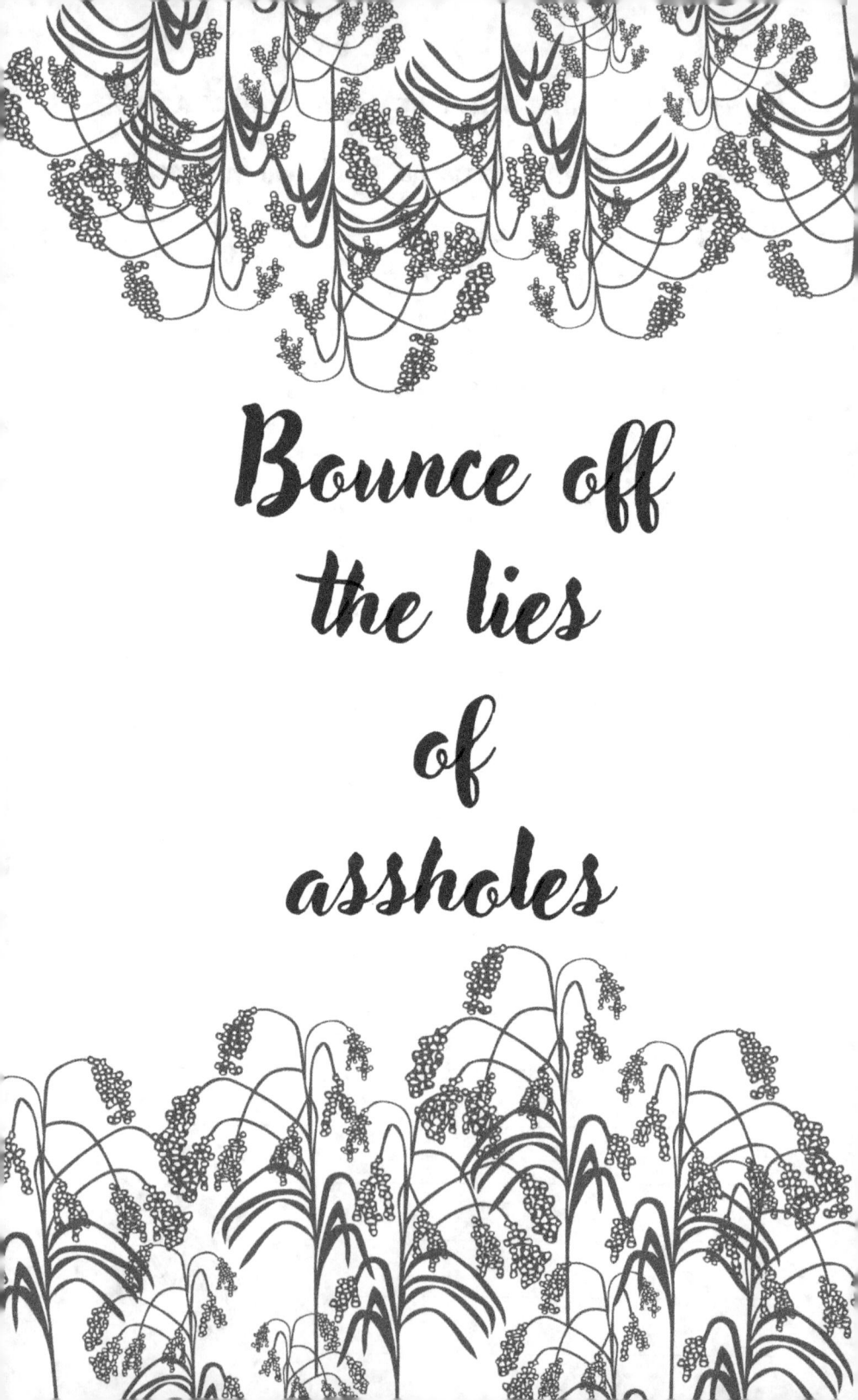

If someone outright lies about you, what are you going to do about it? Write out a plan.

By all means tell people who make you angry how you fuck feel and what you really think of them

Think of some people who constantly made you angry in your life. What did or would you say to them, or do about it now?

Always safeguard and protect your own fucking truth

What is your real truth? Write about how you feel about yourself and what you truly believe in?

Give yourself extra time when you need it for things of fucking importance

How can you be more patient and productive to accomplish your most important goals?

Remember each day is a beautiful new fucking opportunity

What opportunities do you see around yourself every day? What can you do with them?

Seize the best fucking times when you recognize them

Think about getting the most out of life. What can you do when you recognize the potential of something great? Describe it here.

At times, make yourself fucking brand new

What are some positive ways you can transform yourself? What would that be like? How would you go about it?

When your energy is low, take the time to recharge your fucking batteries

What can you do to recharge yourself? Think of some ways, make a planned list, and get to it!

Love yourself everyday and fuck off to the people who treat you badly

When people treat you badly, what are some ways you can block their negativity and protect yourself with self love and care?

Use self-love
to navigate
your good
fucking fortune

List reasons why you are deserving of good fortune. Describe what that good fortune would be like.

Always
let
fucking
assholes know
the truth
they deserve

Think of ways you can tell the truth to unpleasant and nasty people, even if you don't know them.

Have you ever met an arrogant asshole? How did you deal with this person? Describe it here.

Never let an arrogant asshole belittle your dreams or accomplishments and get away with it

Get rid of that old shit and start fucking over

Want to start something new? What will you get rid of and what will you acquire or do now?

Make everyday as fucking incredible as you possibly can

What makes you feel incredible? Get in touch with yourself and describe a list of those incredible thoughts.

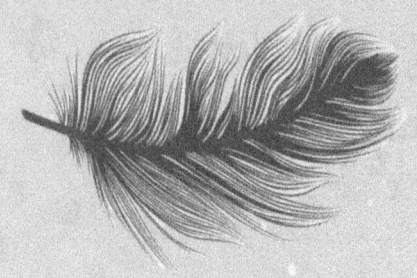

Use your talents to align your goals and get what you really fucking want

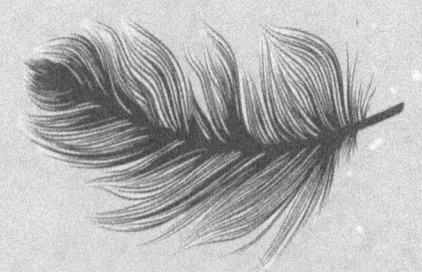

What specific gifts or talents of yours can you use to get the things you want the most in life?

When someone wants you to fail, tell them too bad, that they are bound to fucking fail

How are you going to handle people who want you to fail or are jealous of your plans for success?

When people are fuck nice to you, thank them

How do you react to people who are nice to you? What do you do when they make you feel good?

When you figure out who you are, shit ya, be the best of it

Who are you really? Describe yourself in some detail and your best qualities.

Remember a time when you were afraid or hesitant to be yourself. Why were you? And what did you do about it?

Never apologize for being your authentic and awesome fuck self

Don't
ever
feel
bad
being fucking
honest
with
people

How can you be more genuine with people you actually like? Describe your relationships.

When you are in an uncomfortable situation, fucking do something about it

Describe a situation that is or was very uncomfortable for you. What did you do to make it better?

Never think twice about making your own fucking life choices

How do you make sure that others don't dominate your life choices and decisions?

What are some places you would take a vacation to? Make a list and start making plans.

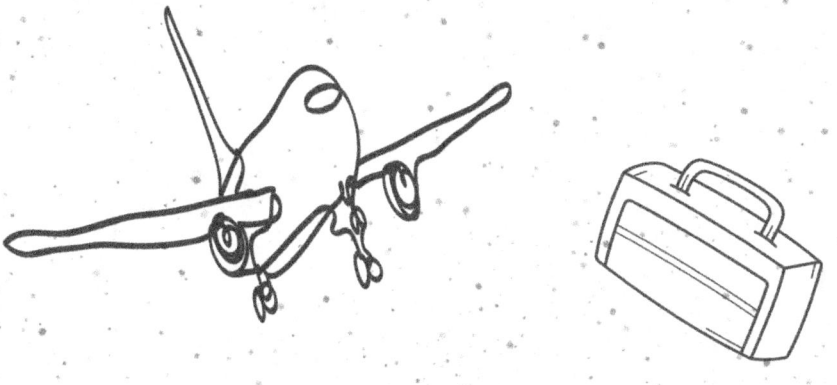

Take a vacation when you fucking need one

Give a compliment or gratitude to someone when they fucking deserve it

Think of people who deserve compliments or gratitude from you. Write something about them.

Get out of your own way when you fucking need to

What are ways you can stop procrastinating about things that are good for you to do?

Have that glass of wine, margarita, or martini and fucking enjoy yourself.

Once in while, indulge yourself with your favorite drinks and foods. Describe what they are?

Time to wear something new. What is it and how does it feel to wear it?

Pay off some
of those fucking
bills and debts
to
free up your
mind from worry

Make a list of things unpaid. Check off the ones that you can pay and celebrate!

Longer term, think about some places that would enrich your spirit and soul. Make a list about them and explain why you chose them?

Let's plan for the fucking trip of a lifetime

Take time out for the salon. What would you do for your hair? What look and what color?

Honor your personal life. What are some things you feel shouldn't be shared with most people?

Remember your personal life is no one's fucking business

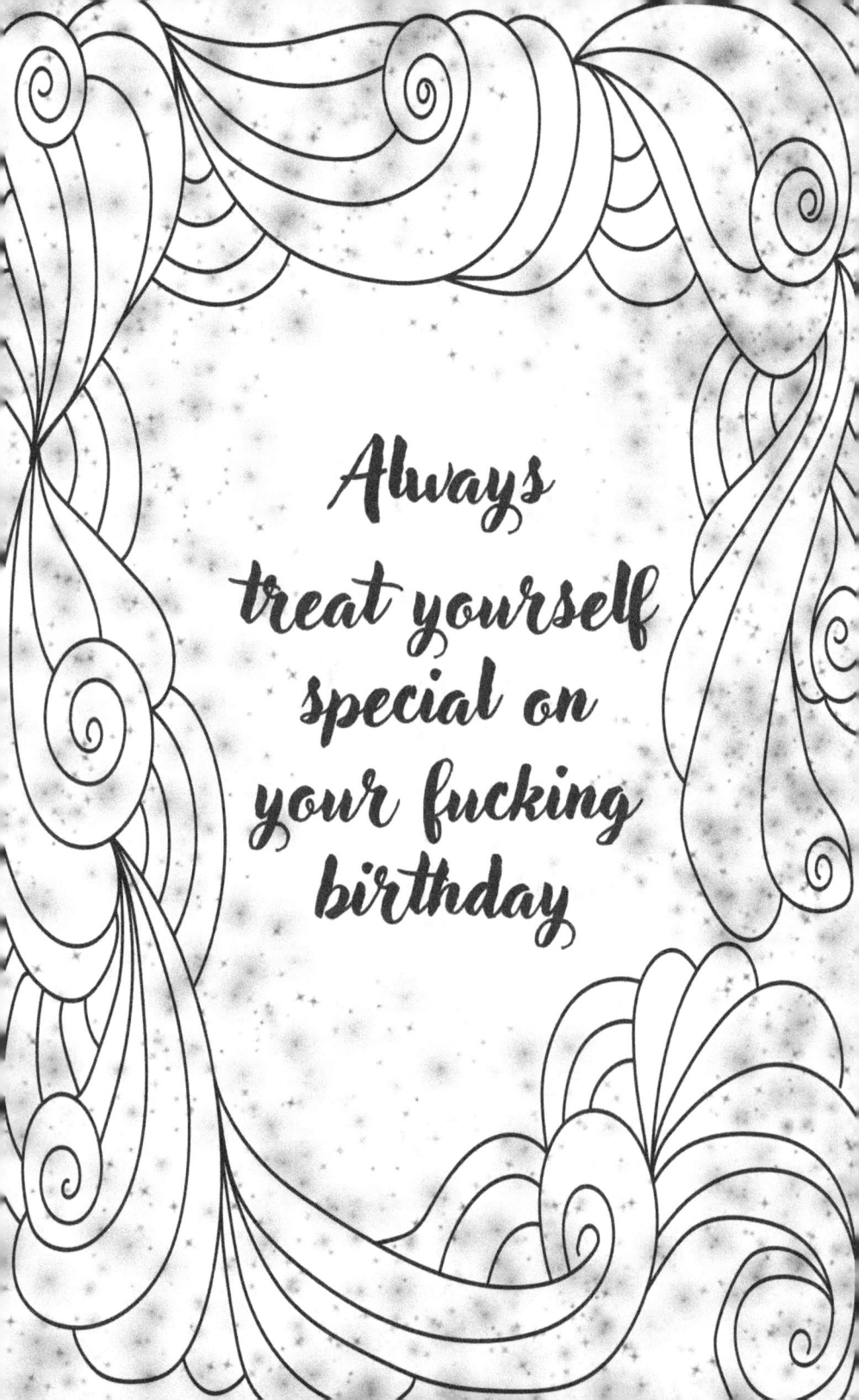

What are you going to do on your next birthday? What are ways you can make it super special?

What would make you feel more alive and in touch with the most beautiful things in life?

Always follow your fucking dreams

Sometimes you have to be extra determined to honor and protect your dreams. How will you go about doing this?

Never let a fucking asshole control your life

When have you felt someone else was too controlling over you and your life? How did they behave? And what happened next?

What are some books you have been wanting to read but haven't made time for? Make a list, describe them, and begin one.

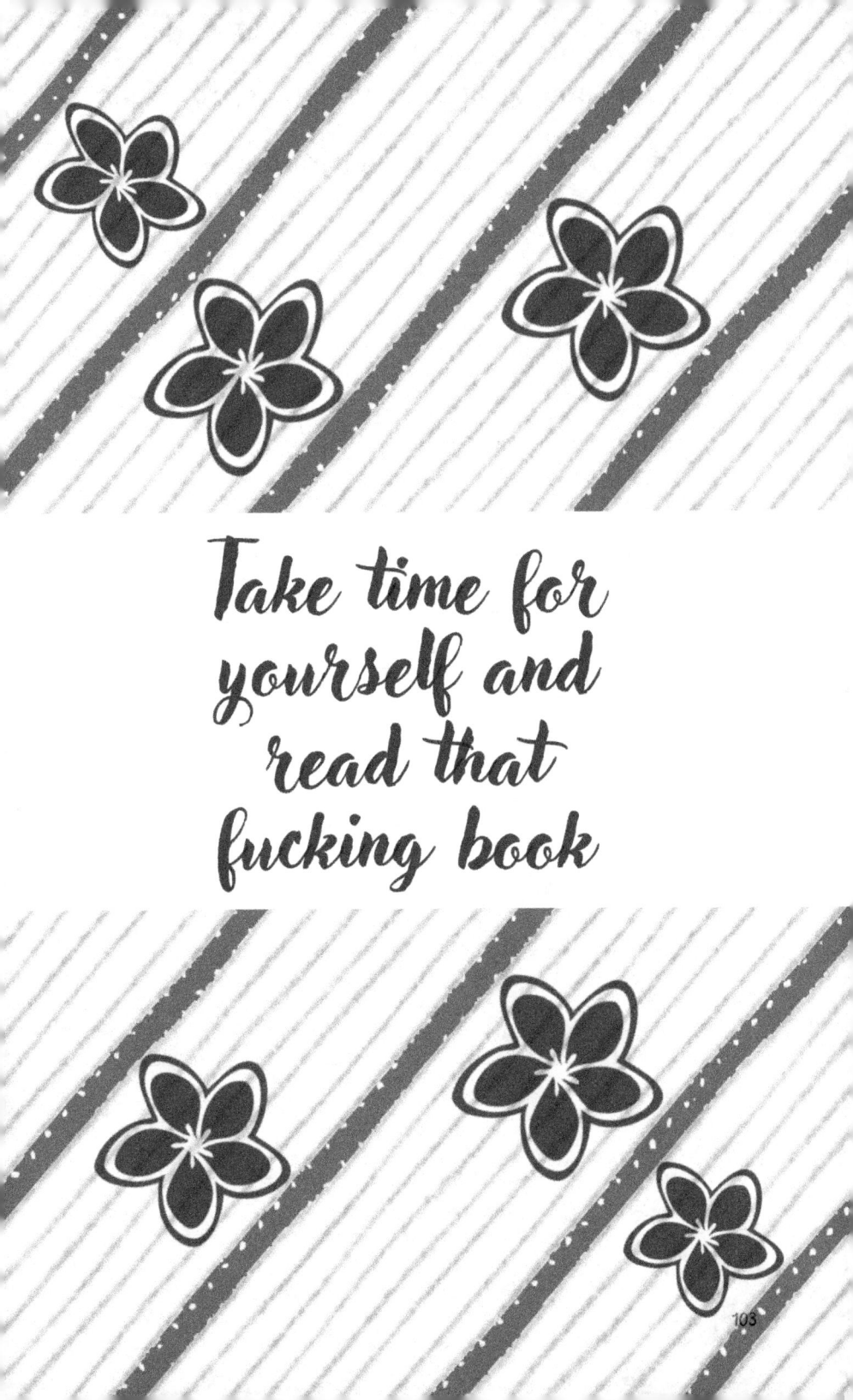

Have you ever wanted to write a story, paint a painting, or learn a new instrument? Describe your desires here.

Go ahead, write that story, paint that picture, or learn that new fucking instrument

Be careful

not to have to

swallow

your fucking pride

Remember a time when you were in the wrong and someone else deserved an apology. Describe what happened and why.

Never give in to an asshole but don't act like a freaking asshole either

Think about another time when you did or didn't give in to an asshole. What happened and how did you improve the situation?

Always believe in yourself and never let others make you feel fucking insecure or incompetent

Remember times when you felt insecure in life. How did or would you deal with the experiences now? Be specific and describe your emotions.

Handle any fucking situation with grace and poise

Think of a situation where you can really shine using grace and poise. Describe what happens.

Let your family know that it's your fucking life

Make a plan to explain to family members that you have your own life to live. Describe it all here.

It's time to
make peace
with your fun
fuck self and
go on with life

Let go of personal regrets. Start all over if you need to, then forgive, release, and write about it.

Keep saying positive fuck it happy go lucky affirmations to yourself

What positive affirmations do you have for yourself? Write them out and speak them daily.

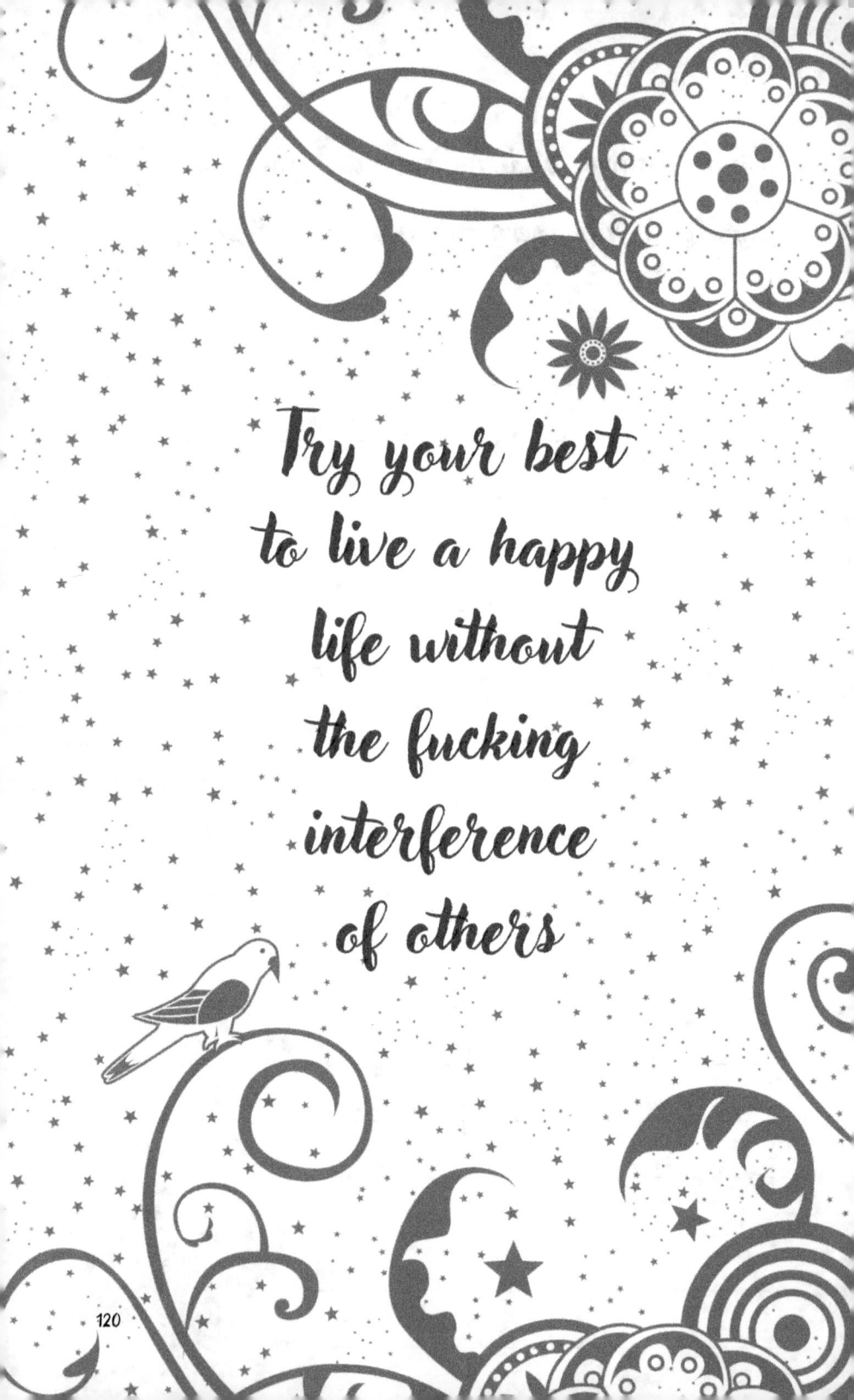

Keep track of your best and happier life by journaling. Continue to write about your latest feelings, goals, and growing progress.

NOW SEIZE YOUR FUCKING SPECIAL HAPPY MOMENTS

ABOUT THE AUTHOR

Mimi Margarita is a created name. Mimi has formal education in art, life coaching, psychology, special needs, writing, and more. She lives in Connecticut and spends her time between Greenwich and New York. Be sure to look for her other books and journals as they become available worldwide.

Additionally, please be kind and take the time to leave a review from where you found this book. Much appreciated. Thank you. Gracias. Merci.

Written or Visual Notes